# MARK TWAIN

## along the Mississippi

### Wayne Youngblood

**WORLD ALMANAC® LIBRARY**

Please visit our web site at: www.worldalmanaclibrary.com
For a free color catalog describing World Almanac® Library's list of high-quality books
and multimedia programs, call 1-800-848-2928 (USA) or 1-800-387-3178 (Canada).
World Almanac® Library's fax: (414) 332-3567.

Library of Congress Cataloging-in-Publication Data

Youngblood, Wayne.
    Mark Twain along the Mississippi / Wayne L. Youngblood.
      p. cm. — (In the footsteps of American heroes)
    Includes bibliographical references and index.
    ISBN 0-8368-6430-1 (lib. bdg.)
    ISBN 0-8368-6435-2 (softcover)
      1. Twain, Mark (1835-1910)—Homes and haunts—Mississippi River—Juvenile
literature.  2. Twain, Mark, (1835-1910)—Knowledge—Pilots and pilotage—Juvenile
literature.  3. Authors, American—19th century—Biography—Juvenile literature.  4. Pilots
and pilotage—Mississippi River—Biography—Juvenile literature.  5. Steamboats—Mississippi
River—History—Juvenile literature.  6. Mississippi River—History—Juvenile literature.
I. Title.  II. Series.
PS1334.Y68  2006
818'.409—dc22
[B]
                                                                     2005054472

First published in 2006 by
**World Almanac® Library**
A Member of the WRC Media Family of Companies
330 West Olive Street, Suite 100
Milwaukee, WI 53212 USA

Copyright © 2006 by World Almanac® Library.

Produced by Compendium Publishing Ltd
First Floor, 43 Frith Street
London W1D 4SA

For Compendium Publishing
Editors: Don Gulbrandsen and Joe Hollander
Picture research: Mindy Day and Sandra Forty
Design: Ian Hughes/Compendium Design
Artwork: Mark Franklin

World Almanac® Library managing editor: Valerie J. Weber
World Almanac® Library editor: Leifa Butrick
World Almanac® Library art direction: Tammy West
World Almanac® Library production: Jessica Morris and Robert Kraus

Photo credits: CORBIS: all except; Library of Congress: pages 14, 42 (both); Getty Images: 33, 40.

Printed in the United States of America

1 2 3 4 5 6 7 8 9 10 09 08 07 06

# CONTENTS

*COVER:* Writer, riverboat pilot, and famous lecturer, Mark Twain traveled throughout the United States and world—and wrote about much of it.

*TITLE PAGE:* By the time this picture was taken in about 1890, Samuel Clemens had become a famous writer under his pen name, Mark Twain.

# INTRODUCTION

"**S**team-boat a-comin'!" In the nineteenth century, this cry was an important signal in river towns across the United States. The approaching steamboat would often carry mail, travelers, and much-needed supplies destined for the town. The steamboat was a link to the outside; for dwellers of small towns, it was a symbol of a large, exciting world that they knew was just out of sight beyond the river's next bend. During this time, no person did as much to celebrate the romance of the steamboat—and of travel, adventure, and freedom—as the most well loved author in the United States, Mark Twain.

Mark Twain was known variously as W. Epaminandas Adrastas Blab, Thomas Jefferson Snodgrass, Josh Muggins, and Rambler; but he was born in 1835 as Samuel Clemens. Clemens never really intended to become famous, but he wanted to be rich and to have lots of adventures. His ability to assess human nature and describe people honestly and humorously allowed him to touch the lives of millions of people during his lifetime and hundreds of millions of people since

**Mark Twain in 1903, wearing his trademark white suit**

**Mark Twain in the 1870s**

his death. He was finest writer of "nonfiction fiction" in the United States. He wrote numerous fictional stories, but many of them were based on real-life experiences—particularly those stories written about the Mississippi River.

At the peak of his career, Twain was more than just a writer. He traveled around the world as a popular lecturer, sharing humorous stories with appreciative audiences. He was acclaimed, and his likeness was more recognizable to many United States citizens than the faces of U.S. presidents. Inventor Thomas Alva Edison once said, "The average American loves his family. If he has any love left over for some other person, he generally selects Mark Twain." When President Franklin Delano Roosevelt was making plans for the recovery of the nation from the Great Depression, he found the phrase "New Deal" in Twain's book, *A Connecticut Yankee in King Arthur's Court*. The country is filled with Mark Twain banks, diners, smoke shops, cigars, and schools; scores of products and businesses have been named after this beloved American. More than 6,500,000 Internet web sites feature his name prominently.

In January 1940, the U.S. Post Office issued the first of a new portrait series of postage stamps entitled "Famous Americans." Samuel L. Clemens was such a famous author that his pen name of Mark Twain did not need to be included on the stamp.

Other famous authors pay homage to this master of words. In *Green Hills of Africa*, Ernest Hemingway wrote: "All modern American literature comes from one book by Mark Twain called *Huckleberry Finn*. . . . It's the best book we've had. All American writing comes from that. There was nothing before. There has been nothing as good since." At all scholastic levels, Twain's best works are still assigned more often than other books. They are among the best-loved stories worldwide—particularly *Tom Sawyer* and *The Adventures of Huckleberry Finn*, both books that deal with the adventures of boys who lived near the Mississippi River during its heyday as a shipping route in the mid-nineteenth century.

Of course, there is much more to the man than his writing. Twain lived in a remarkable time. He saw the Mississippi River as America's Main Street at its finest.

He endured the Civil War. He traveled to the western frontier. He visited the Hawaiian Islands before most people had ever heard of them and crossed the Atlantic Ocean twenty-five times during an era when many people never even left the state of their birth. He was one of the first authors ever to use a typewriter (a new-fangled contraption invented during the 1870s) and had one of the earliest private telephones. During his lifetime, he either met or befriended many literary greats, celebrities, and politicians. He spent time with presidents, kings, emperors, and—of course—common men and women.

One of the most-noted facts about Samuel Clemens is that his birth and death coincided with the appearance of Halley's Comet—a huge event for people living during those times. It seems particularly ironic that Clemens is unquestionably better known now than the comet.

The main locations mentioned in the text are featured on this map with present-day state boundaries. The numbers identify sites related to Mark Twain that are detailed in the Places to Visit and Research section of this book on page 58. The green dots indicate sites that are discussed in the sidebars.

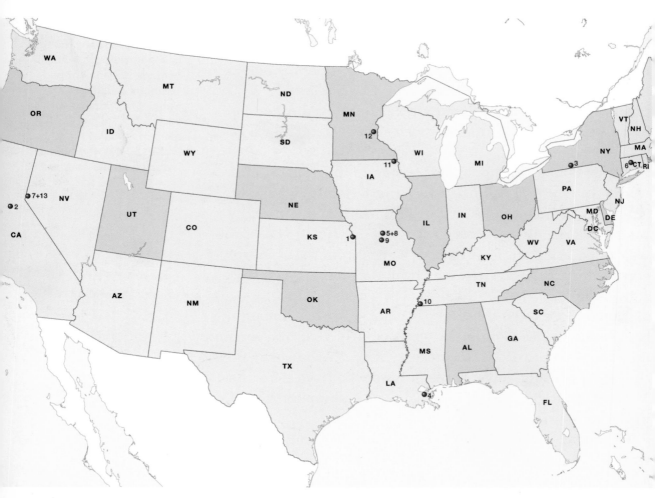

Mark Twain with longtime friend John T. Lewis in 1903. They first met when Lewis risked his own safety to save some of Twain's relatives. The two became firm friends, and Twain used Lewis as a model for the character of the runaway slave Jim in his novel *Huckleberry Finn*.

# CHAPTER 1
# THE EARLY YEARS

Other than for the birth of Samuel Clemens, the year 1835 was not an important one, as world history goes. In the United States, under our nation's ninth president (Andrew Jackson), U.S. citizens were in the midst of the Industrial Revolution and starting to enjoy the conveniences of modern life. The wrench and propeller appeared in 1835, along with two other far-reaching inventions: the telegraph and daguerreotype photography. By the end of the nineteenth century, these two items would change the lives of virtually every United States citizen. Among the important events of the year was the Texas revolt against Mexico, beginning with the battle of the Alamo.

On the Mississippi River, the steamboat was in its prime. Steam power had been introduced to the river in 1811, and trade grew steadily, until the Mississippi became the virtual lifeline of the nation.

Halley's Comet reappeared during the year, and Samuel Clemens (Mark Twain) was born on November 30. In his own words, "I was born the 30th of November, 1835, in the almost invisible village of Florida, Monroe County, Missouri. . . . The village contained a hundred people and I increased the population by 1 per cent. It is more than many of the best men in history could have done for a town. . . . There is no record of a person doing as much—not even Shakespeare. But I did it for Florida, Missouri, and it shows I could have done it for any place—even London, I suppose."

"Sam's" birthplace was a two-room house that was not much more than a shack. His aunt and uncle, Patsy and John Quarles, had moved to Florida, Missouri, in the early 1830s and thought their future there would be bright. They

# THE MISSISSIPPI RIVER

At the time of Mark Twain's birth, the Mississippi River was truly America's Main Street. The Mississippi (an Indian name meaning "big river") starts as a small trickle in northern Minnesota. Glaciers dug the riverbed, which in some places reaches a depth of more than 100 feet (30 meters). At its widest point (near Cairo, Illinois), the river is about 4,500 feet (1,371 m) across. The Mississippi travels some 2,350 miles (3,781 kilometers), neatly splitting the country into eastern and western sections. Along the way, the river collects water from countless streams and rivers, including other major arteries, such as the Missouri, Ohio, and Arkansas Rivers. In 1811, steam-powered vessels came to the river. That year also marked the New Madrid, Missouri, earthquake, which was so violent it made the Mississippi run backward in some places and changed its course in others. With the advent of steamboats, the river became the single most important artery of trade for America. By the time Twain was born in 1835, the river was a great, bustling highway. It is no wonder Americans tapped into this powerful mode of transportation early in the country's history, and why it is still so valuable. By the time Twain wrote about the river in the 1880s, it was largely bridled by bridges, and the heyday of the steamboat was over. He wrote, "Mississippi steamboating was born about 1812; at the end of thirty years it had grown to mighty proportions; and in less than thirty years more it was dead; A strangely short life for so majestic a creature." A wonderful place to learn more about the Mississippi River and life along it is the National Mississippi River Museum and Aquarium in Dubuque, Iowa (map reference 11). The large facility has numerous exhibits devoted to the natural and human history of the great river. The Fred W. Woodward Riverboat Museum that is part of the complex tells the story of the great steamers that plied the river, the same boats that Samuel Clemens piloted.

Greer Springs, Mark Twain National Forest, Missouri.

convinced Patsy's sister, Jane, and her husband, John Clemens, to move there from Tennessee in mid-1835. Samuel was born shortly after their arrival in Missouri, and his brother Henry was born three years later. A few months after the death of Samuel's older sister Margaret in 1839, the family moved to Hannibal, Missouri, but they came back to visit and stay at the Quarles's farm nearly every summer thereafter.

**Book illustration of Tom Sawyer, Twain's immortal creation. Twain used happy memories of his own childhood in his tales of Tom Sawyer. As he later remarked, "None of these happy memories, however, took place inside a schoolhouse."**

# Twain's Family and Early Life

Samuel Langhorne Clemens was the fifth child born to John and Jane Clemens. Samuel was his grandfather's name, and Langhorne was the name of a family friend. John Clemens owned a small store and provided legal services. "The Judge," as he was known, was anxious to support his family and, ultimately, become wealthy. He tried any trade he felt he could manage. He also was an inventor of sorts and created numerous gadgets, all of which failed to catch on. In 1839, when Samuel was only four, John packed up his family and moved to Hannibal, Missouri, which was about 30 miles (48 km) northwest of the town of Florida. He opened a grocery store.

Clemens's mother was much kinder than his rather distant father, and she had quite a sense of humor. It served her well when dealing with young Samuel, who was mischievous, to say the least. When one of Samuel's friends had the measles (which were sometimes fatal at the time), he climbed into bed with the friend in an effort to catch them. He did. Soon he had red spots all over his body and a dangerous fever. Family friends made their way to the Clemens's home to pay their last respects, but Samuel got better. When he later asked his mother about his illness, Clemens said, "I suppose you were afraid I wouldn't live." Jane, with a twinkle in her eye, simply quipped, "I was afraid you would." In remembering his life later, Clemens wrote, "My childhood was filled with warm and wonderful memories." He added, "None of these happy memories, however, took place inside a schoolhouse." That is where some of his childhood problems began.

By the time young Samuel was school-aged, formal education was available for children for the cost of twenty cents per week. Lessons included reading, writing, arithmetic, Bible studies, spelling, and good manners. His teacher was a woman named Mrs. Elizabeth Horr, who was, by today's standards, a harsh taskmaster. On his very first day at school (at the age of five), young Samuel forgot to stand when he was asked to recite. Mrs. Horr told him that if it happened again, he would be whipped. He made the same mistake later in the day and was sent

## MARK TWAIN BIRTHPLACE STATE HISTORICAL SITE

The two-room cabin in which Samuel Clemens was born is still standing, but it has been moved about a quarter mile and is now enclosed within a modern museum at Mark Twain State Park (map reference 5 and 8). A monument marks the original site of the cabin in Florida, Missouri. The museum features exhibits about Twain's life and even a handwritten manuscript of *The Adventures of Tom Sawyer.* The adjacent 2,775-acre (1,123-hectare) state park preserves the beautiful landscape in which the Clemens family lived when Samuel was born in 1835.

## SAMUEL CLEMENS'S FRIENDS

Samuel's closest friends as a young boy were Laura Hawkins and Tom Blankenship. These two later served as the inspiration for fictional character Tom Sawyer's friends Becky Thatcher and Huck Finn. Hawkins was a freckle-faced classmate who lifted Clemens's spirits. Blankenship, who was four years older than Clemens, seemed to live without a care in the world—though his home life left much to be desired. Blankenship's parents spent most of their time in taverns drinking, while Tom, dressed in rags, slept in a barrel near the Clemens's house. Because of his background, Tom was thought to be a poor influence on the children of Hannibal, and they were urged to stay away from him. This parental disapproval of Blankenship only made him more popular; and he taught the other children how to smoke corncob pipes, search for turtle eggs, curse, and other skills a mischievous child needed. Other friends of Clemens included Will Bowen and John Briggs.

Once, when Clemens was nine, he was caught skipping school. His punishment was to whitewash the tall fence that surrounded his family's yard. Samuel tired quickly of the task, and when Will and John happened to pass by, he quickly formulated a plan. With grand sweeps, he began painting the fence as if doing so was great fun and started to whistle loudly. Within moments, the boys were "allowed" to paint the fence. Others showed up and traded Clemens worms, frogs, apple cores, doorknobs, and other treasures for the privilege of taking a turn to whitewash the fence. This real-life incident became one of the most popular vignettes in all of Clemens's writing.

*Tom Sawyer Washing the Fence*, an illustration from *The Adventures of Tom Sawyer*.

outside to choose a suitable switch (stick). When he returned with a rotten old stick, the punishment was not lessened, and he was ordered to choose a strong switch. This was just the first of many whippings the young boy received. Clemens was bored with school and broke more rules than Horr could create.

Later in life, echoing his mother's comments, Clemens wrote, "I was fortunate to survive my childhood, although there are some folks who might think my survival was unfortunate."

# Living on the Mississippi

The move to Hannibal significantly affected the rest of Mark Twain's life. Hannibal, a small town at the time, was tucked between two bluffs right on the Mississippi River. Nonetheless, it was much larger than the town of Florida, and because of its proximity to the center of the nation's trade—the mighty Mississippi—it had a much higher incidence of crime and odd occurrences. Many of them eventually became the subjects of Twain's writing. Probably the most consistently exciting aspect of town life at the time was signaled with the words "Steam-boat a-comin'!" This served as the rallying cry for villagers to crowd down to the dock to see what (or who) the boat would bring. "The sound of that riverboat's whistle raised goosebumps as big as walnuts on me," Clemens once wrote. Tobacco, molasses and sugar, fabrics, pork barrels, and all kinds of other exotic merchandise would be unloaded in a scant ten minutes or so; then the steamboat was once again chugging its way up or down the river.

In this 1902 photograph, author Mark Twain stands near a group of people outside his old home in Hannibal (map reference 9).

Other favorite activities for a young boy on the river included swimming in Bear Creek (Clemens nearly drowned three times) and exploring the numerous caves and bluffs along the river. He also loved visiting his uncle's farm near Florida, where he played with eight cousins and numerous slave children. One thing that young Samuel noted was that there was a difference between black and white children. "We were comrades and not comrades," he wrote. A complete friendship between the children was impossible due to their very different lives.

There was a darker side of life in Hannibal, too. Because of its position on the Mississippi, all types of people arrived in the town. Violence was always present. During his childhood, Clemens saw a hanging, several murders, and a man burned to death in jail. He encountered a corpse in his father's office and witnessed the drowning of several friends. Of course, these experiences also served him well in later years as he wrote about them.

*Above:* **J. M. Clemens's (Twain's father) law office, Hill Street, Hannibal, Marion County, Missouri. Today it is the Twain Bookshop (map reference 9).**

## Apprenticing as a Printer

During Samuel's childhood, the family moved several times—each time to a smaller and less expensive home, thanks to their increasing financial difficulties. Samuel contributed what he could to the family by making deliveries and doing chores for local businesses. He hoped that if he made enough money, his parents would let him quit school. He wasn't so fortunate, however.

On March 24, 1847, when Samuel wasn't quite twelve, his father died of pneumonia. Samuel was not close to his father, but he took his death very hard. He knew his father had struggled with poverty and was deeply in debt, and he worried that he, too, would "follow that same path." This fear of poverty dogged Clemens the rest of his life.

At the time of his father's death, Samuel's oldest brother, Orion, was working as a printer in St. Louis, and he regularly sent money home to help his struggling family. Convinced the printing trade would help his family, young Clemens obtained part-time work at the *Hannibal Gazette* newspaper. He was allowed to quit school entirely in June 1848 to apprentice with Joseph Ament at the *Missouri Courier* newspaper, also in Hannibal. As an apprentice, young Clemens was not paid. He was given lodging, food, and clothes and, in that way, was able to remove the burden of his care from his mother. The life of an apprentice was not fun. He slept on a straw mattress and ate skimpy meals (when he wasn't stealing potatoes and onions from the basement). His clothes were Ament's hand-me-downs, described by Clemens as giving "me the uncomfortable feeling of living in a circus tent." He commented that "I had to turn up his pants to my ears to make them short enough." Nonetheless, Clemens was able to see how reporters and newspapermen lived and worked. He read their stories as he set them in type and learned much about the world. He dreamed of various adventures and was convinced that newspaper work was the life for him.

During the summer of 1850, Orion returned to Hannibal with a printing press and opened the *Western Union* newspaper. Samuel quit his job at the *Courier* the next year to work for Orion, alongside his younger brother

*Opposite:* **Samuel Clemens's bedroom in the Mark Twain Boyhood Home, Hannibal, Missouri (map reference 9)**

## HANNIBAL, MISSOURI

People all over the world probably have an image in their minds of what Hannibal, Missouri, looks like—even though they've never visited the town—because Samuel Clemens used the town as the setting for *The Adventures of Tom Sawyer* and *The Adventures of Huckleberry Finn*. Today the town boasts several attractions that can be visited on an easy walking tour, including an Interpretive Center (map reference 9), the Mark Twain Boyhood Home and Museum, the Becky Thatcher House, John M. Clemens Justice of the Peace Office, and Grant's Drugstore/Pilaster House. The Clemens family lived for a time in the latter structure, and Samuel's father died in one of the upstairs rooms.

**Mark Twain boyhood home in Hannibal, Missouri, showing the famous fence**

**Statues of Tom Sawyer and Huckleberry Finn amid flower gardens decorate Cardiff Hill (map reference 9), made famous in Twain's book, *Hannibal, Missouri*.**

Henry. Orion's business luck was never much better than his father's. A fire burned some of his equipment, advertisers refused to pay their bills, and a cow chewed up two rollers on the press. Undaunted, Orion bought another paper, the *Hannibal Journal*, in 1852 and combined the two newspapers. In the new publication, he published not only the news but literature and articles about controversial topics such as slavery, the rights of states, and the expansion of America's railway system. Samuel wanted to see more humor and local news, but Orion wasn't interested. Subscriptions lagged.

When Orion went to Tennessee in 1852, he left Samuel in charge of the paper. The younger Clemens, who by now had had two pieces published in eastern publications, quickly added a made-up gossip column to add humor. The column was penned by one W. Epaminandas Adrastas Blab, probably Clemens's first pen name. The circulation of the paper grew steadily, until Orion returned and was furious with young Clemens's changes. In 1853, however, Orion promoted Clemens and gave him his own column to write; but within a few months, the paper's fortunes continued to slide. Samuel, now seventeen, decided it was time to leave home.

**A sign marks the entrance to Mark Twain's Cave (map reference 9), made famous in *The Adventures of Tom Sawyer*, Hannibal, Missouri.**

# CHAPTER 2

# LEAVING MISSOURI TO SEE THE WORLD

Armed with only a little money and a big desire for adventure, Clemens left Hannibal in June 1853, bound for New York City. He especially wanted to see the Crystal Palace at the first international fair in the United States. By the time he reached St. Louis, however, Clemens was out of cash. To raise some money to continue his adventure, Samuel stayed with his sister Pamela and her husband and set type for the *St. Louis Evening News* paper.

In August, he packed up again and headed east. He arrived in New York with thirteen dollars in his pocket and immediately went to the fair, which had an average daily attendance that was twice the number of people who lived in Hannibal. Samuel wrote regular accounts of his visits to the fair and sent them to his brother Orion, who published them in the *Hannibal Journal*. Readers loved his writing, and he continued to write about the fair. To support himself in the big city, Samuel found a printing job that paid enough to allow him to rent a room at a cheap boarding house. He spent most of his free time in a nearby library, where he became a voracious reader. He took in all the history and fine literature he could devour. He also made frequent visits to the theater.

Soon, however, Samuel began feeling enclosed by the big city and its crowds. He left New York in the fall of 1853, but his available money took him only as far as Philadelphia, where he found work at the *Philadelphia Enquirer* newspaper. In November he found out that Orion and his mother had moved to Muscatine, Iowa, where his brother had bought another newspaper, the *Muscatine Journal*. Orion let Samuel know he had a job waiting for him if he wanted it.

**Samuel Clemens stands in front of his old home in Hannibal, Missouri, (map reference 9) on June 6, 1902. He left Hannibal in 1853.**

By late summer 1854, eighteen-year-old Samuel was happy to be back with his family (although he doubted that the paper would survive under his brother's leadership). Adventure could temporarily wait. In December, Orion was married. He promised his new wife they would move to Keokuk, Iowa, if the Muscatine paper failed. By March, it became clear that Orion could make good on his promise, because the paper was failing miserably. Orion was still convinced that his place was in the publishing field, and he took over the Ben Franklin Book and Job Office in Keokuk. He invited Samuel and his mother along. Soon after, Samuel read an article about the rich cocoa plantations in South America, and he became convinced that was the place he should be. He began fantasizing about his South American adventures, even though he knew next to nothing about the continent.

One October morning in 1856, Samuel found something stuck to the bottom of his shoe. It was a $50 bill! He thought the lucky find was a sign he should go to South America. To soothe his conscience, Samuel took out a newspaper ad to find the owner of the money. "I didn't describe it particularly," Clemens later recalled, "and I waited in daily fear that the owner would turn up and take away my good fortune." Fortunately no one claimed the money, so Samuel purchased a railroad ticket to Cincinnati, presumably his first stop on his way to South America. From there he would catch a steamboat south. He also agreed to write (for five dollars each) travel letters for the *Keokuk Post* newspaper from the perspective of a country bumpkin. He signed these letters "Thomas Jefferson Snodgrass."

## AMERICA'S FIRST INTERNATIONAL FAIR

Just two years after the very first World's Fair in London (1851), Horace Greeley, Phineas T. Barnum, and a group of investors organized the first international fair in the United States, the Great Exhibition of Art and Industry, held in New York City in 1853. The centerpiece of this exhibition was the New York Crystal Palace, a large iron-and-glass dome (shaped like a Greek cross, with all arms of equal length) in which the exposition was housed. The location, where present-day Bryant Park and the New York Public Library now stand, was then on the outskirts of the city. The fair opened July 14, 1853, with the commemoration of the Crystal Palace. The next day, President Franklin Pierce inaugurated the event. Secretary of War Jefferson Davis (who would later become president of the Confederate States during the Civil War) also attended.

During the months the fair was open, it drew people from all over the country, and many local papers ran news of the event as they received it from correspondents. Young Samuel Clemens was fascinated with the Crystal Palace and vowed to see it.

Despite the enormous popularity of the fair and its effect on the imaginations of citizens across the country, it was a financial failure. The palace leaked, ruining exhibits, and there was financial mismanagement. Nonetheless, it provided the incentive for young Clemens to begin his travels.

The Crystal Palace was built in 1853 for the second World's Fair, which was held at Bryant Park, New York. Well over one million people flocked to see the attractions, including the first working elevator in the world.

# CHAPTER 3

# THE LURE OF THE MISSISSIPPI

On April 15, 1857, twenty-one-year-old Samuel Clemens was ready to begin his journey—a journey he thought would take him to the rich cocoa fields and unexplored regions of the Amazon River in South America. He boarded what he termed an "ancient tub," the *Paul Jones*, in Cincinnati (with thirty dollars still in his pocket). It traveled westward on the Ohio River and then headed south on the Mississippi to New Orleans. Clemens then planned to travel to South America by unknown means. He was so excited by the trip, he felt he had become "the subject of his own admiration." "I was a traveler!" Clemens wrote. "A word never had tasted so good in my mouth before."

Not unlike many young so-called explorers, Samuel did not know much about the location or nature of Brazil, and he did not have much of a plan to get there. He thought he could find odd jobs along the way to finance the trip. On the trip to New Orleans, he strolled the boat's boiler deck, pretending to be a world traveler, and spent time (after being rebuffed by the first mate) listening to the tales told by the night watchman. The adventures related by this watchman—bloodshed, narrow escapes, and various personal wrongs—became increasingly incredible. "I sat speechless, enjoying, shuddering, wondering, worshiping," Clemens wrote. The tales continued to get more fantastic until Clemens realized he had been had. These events no doubt contributed to his later ability to tell a good tale. He also closely followed the activities of the men in the pilothouse, eventually striking up conversations with Captain Horace Bixby, a veteran steamboat pilot.

## EXPLORING THE MISSISSIPPI TODAY

The modern Mississippi is much changed from Samuel Clemens's days on the river. A series of locks and dams controls the flow and depth of the river and makes it easy for giant barges to move cargo up and down the great stream. That said, the Mississippi is still an exciting place to visit and a popular public waterway. Any size boat—even a canoe—can travel the river and is allowed to pass through the locks. The river is large, unpredictable, and dangerous, however. The massive barges can swamp a small boat in a matter of seconds.

A better way to explore the Mississippi is to travel the river in style. A number of excursion companies offer trips on the river. Modern paddle wheelers such as the *Delta Queen*, the *American Queen*, and the *Mississippi Queen* harken back to the classic fancy riverboats of the nineteenth century and visit ports throughout the Mississippi basin (map reference 4).

The *Delta Queen* is an authentic modern Mississippi paddle wheel riverboat such as Twain would recognize.

After much begging by Clemens, Bixby finally allowed him to take the wheel for a moment—a moment that forever changed Clemens's life. He never made it to South America. As he held the *Paul Jones*'s wheel, Clemens's childhood fantasies of becoming a riverboat pilot took over. Suddenly, to Clemens, the world of the riverboat pilot was the best thing he could imagine. The power, freedom, and independence were obvious. By the time the *Paul Jones* arrived in New Orleans (and after a few more times at the wheel in broad, deep stretches of the river), Clemens's love of the riverboat had taken over.

Clemens found out that not only was there no scheduled voyage to Para, Brazil (his desired destination), there might not be another for "ten to twelve years." It did not take long for young Clemens to banish all thoughts of going to South America and focus completely on becoming a Mississippi riverboat pilot. His decision was reinforced by the fact that "the nine or ten dollars still left in my pocket would not suffice for so imposing an exploration as I had planned." He pleaded with Bixby to teach him the trade. Bixby was not terribly thrilled with the idea and even pointed out to young Clemens that cub pilots generally not only paid a stiff fee (at least $500) to learn the craft, but that they frequently worked for up to eighteen months, earning nothing more than food and a place to sleep. Furthermore, many never became good enough to earn the license. Undaunted, an excited Clemens offered $100 down, with the remainder to be paid from his

**Swamp on the Mississippi by Joseph Rusling Meeker in 1871**

wages once he was licensed. Although Bixby had to wait for this first payment until they reached St. Louis (and Clemens could borrow the money from his brother-in-law, William Moffett), he consented to teach the eager young man. In his inexperienced mind, Clemens felt that all one needed to do to be a pilot was to keep the boat in the water, "and I did not consider that that could be much of a trick, since it was so wide." He did not realize that the Mississippi River was a dangerous place, with many turns and obstacles that changed as frequently as the weather.

On April 30, 1857, the Amazon dream was officially dead, as Bixby and Clemens began the trip northward from New Orleans. Early on the first trip to St. Louis, Bixby handed the wheel over to Clemens saying, "Here. Take her, and shave those steamboats as close as you'd peel an apple." Clemens did not follow this order, choosing instead to give the other boats wide berth, thinking it safer. Bixby angrily

**Ships and boats crowd the water of the Mississippi River at New Orleans in 1872.**

23

took the wheel and, as Twain later put it, "trimmed the ships so closely that disaster seemed ceaselessly imminent." He was not being careless; he was giving Clemens a lesson in handling a boat with the fine precision necessary to get it out of tight scrapes. Bixby knew that the "easy" or current near the shore was best for boats destined upstream. Pilots did not have to fight the current as much so they hugged the shore going upstream, even though there was apparently plenty of river to go around.

Bixby had agreed to teach Clemens the river between New Orleans and St. Louis— roughly a 1,300-mile (2,092-km) stretch—and he fully intended for Samuel to learn every bend, every

*Below: Celebrated Race of the Steamers Robert E. Lee and Natchez.* **An 1883 illustration of a race that took place from New Orleans to St. Louis in June 1870. The *Robert E. Lee* won the race by several hours.**

**Map of the Mississippi showing feeder rivers and major steamboat ports**

snag, every island, every sandbar, and every current—both in daylight and at night. He also had to learn to avoid the wrecks of boats that had not been careful enough. The stretch between New Orleans and St. Louis alone contained more than five hundred treacherous shoals (shallows) that had already claimed more than twenty steamboats. Clemens kept a notebook in which he recorded all the details he observed. While this was an important process, it had its downside. Because riverboat pilots worked

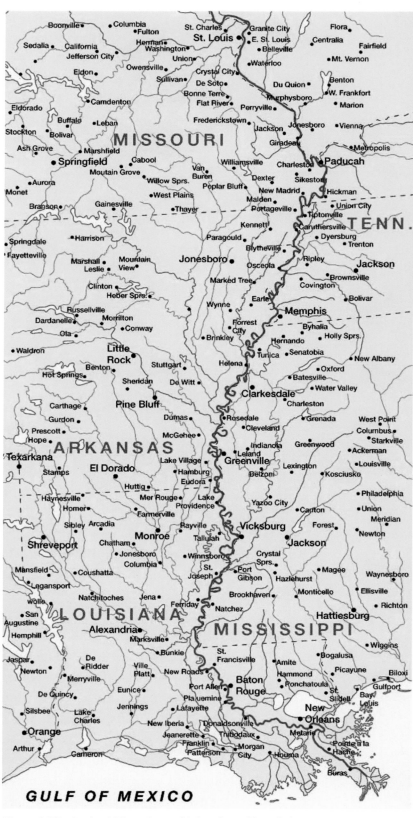

**Map of Mississippi River from St. Louis to New Orleans**

**Late nineteenth-century painting of Samuel Clemens**

four-hour shifts, there were significant information gaps in his journals, with no guarantee that he would be on duty for specific stretches of the river that he needed to learn. Another complicating factor was the fact that a boat acts very differently going downstream when the current is behind it than when it is going upstream heading into the flow. Thus, Clemens had two 1,300-mile (2092-km) rivers to memorize.

When they arrived in St. Louis, Bixby and Clemens left the *Paul Jones* and signed on to a much larger, fancier New Orleans-based steamer, the *Crescent City*. This boat came complete with oil paintings, a long saloon, brass spittoon (instead of an old box filled with sawdust), and waiters who brought them snacks during their watch. The pilothouse was enclosed in glass, with a sofa and red and gold window curtains. Best of all, the servants called the young Clemens "sir." Despite the relative luxury, Clemens occasionally felt disheartened. He was rapidly learning that a riverboat pilot's job was far more complex than he could ever have imagined. For example, the lower Mississippi was loaded with horseshoe-shaped turns created through geologic events over centuries. Some of these bends were so pronounced, Clemens noted, that if passengers were to leave the boat and walk across the land at the narrowest point, they could reach the other side and then relax for several hours waiting for the steamboat to catch up.

Along with learning the river came learning the terminology of the boatmen. For Clemens's purpose, the most significant of these words were those involved in

## RIVERBOAT PILOTS

During the nineteenth century, Samuel Clemens and thousands of other young boys dreamed of being riverboat pilots. These men, considered the most elite of those who plied the river, did a vital job. They literally held the lives of all passengers in their hands as they steered their boats. Not even the captain gave them orders. Furthermore, they were well-paid for this responsibility, making as much as $250 per month, a very high salary during this era. When riverboat pilots were not on duty, they cut a dashing figure in all the exotic cities they visited. A typical outfit included kid gloves (made of fine leather), patent-leather boots, silk hats, and diamond breast pins on fancy starched shirts. Many were also fine storytellers.

Today, being a Mississippi River boat pilot is still an important job, though quite different than it was during Mark Twain's time. Today, pilots guide powerful diesel tugs that push giant barges that haul coal, grain, oil, and other bulk commodities up and down the river. The Mississippi's locks and dams have stabilized the river and made it easier to navigate, but pilots still have to learn the river and know all the potential hazards between the mouth at New Orleans and the upper limits of navigation in Minnesota. For people interested in learning more about being a riverboat pilot, the Science Museum of Minnesota's Mississippi River Gallery (map reference 12) offers an exhibit that allows a person to tour an authentic towboat and test his or her skills as a pilot on a simulated tour of the river.

**Entrance to the Science Museum of Minnesota in St. Paul.**

measuring the depth of the river with a device constructed of lead and twine. The leadsman on the boat would periodically test the river. As he pulled the twine out, he measured by fathoms—1 fathom is 6 feet (1.8 m). To be safe, a riverboat needed to be in water at least two fathoms deep; anything shallower could damage the hull of the boat. Thus, as the leadsman pulled, he would yell the depth. "Mark three!" would mean 3 fathoms, and that all was well. "Mark twain!" or 2 fathoms, was just at the edge of safety—and maybe that's why the term also made a good pen name for Clemens when he became a prominent author and social critic.

# CHAPTER 4
# LEARNING THE RIVER

The most important part of Clemens's early training was learning the shape of the river. One conversation between Bixby and Clemens was particularly telling:

"My boy," said Bixby, "you've got to know the *shape* of the river perfectly. It is all there is left to steer by on a very dark night. Everything else is blotted out and gone. But mind you, it hasn't the same shape in the night that it has in the daytime."

"How on earth am I ever going to learn it then?" Clemens asked.

"How do you follow a hall at home in the dark?" Bixby replied. "Because you know the shape of it. You can't see it."

"Do you mean to say that I've got to know all the million trifling variations of shape in the banks of this interminable river as well as I know the shape of the front hall at home?"

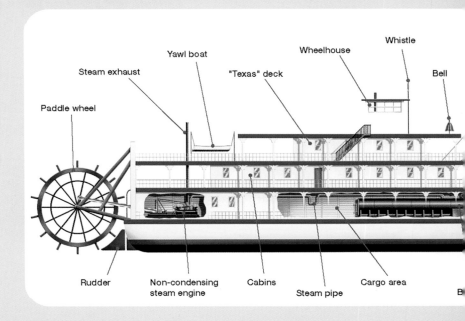

Paddle wheel

Steam exhaust

Yawl boat

"Texas" deck

Wheelhouse

Whistle

Bell

Rudder

Non-condensing steam engine

Cabins

Steam pipe

Cargo area

Bixby replied: "On my honor you've got to know them *better* than any man ever did know the shapes of the halls in his own house."

Any changes in light or visibility, whether it was caused by weather or smoke from villages or from burning sugar-cane waste, distorted the appearance of the river. Seasonal changes complicated matters more, with rising or falling water levels.

Bixby described all the variations of light, weather, and scores of other variables to Clemens. The young pilot-in-training asked if he needed to learn the shape of the river as it was changed by all these factors. Bixby replied, "*No!* You only learn *the* shape of the river; and you learn it with such absolute certainty that you can always steer by the shape that's *in your head*, and never mind the one that's before your eyes." Clemens realized this was an important lesson, one that served him well in many ways throughout his life: Learn your subject so well, you can trust your instincts rather than the illusion of what you see. Of course, even after he learned the shape of the river, constant observation was necessary because the shape changed with flooding, strong storms, and other major events.

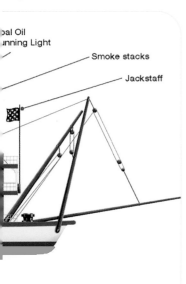

al Oil
unning Light

Smoke stacks

Jackstaff

Clemens became so frustrated with the intense learning process that he told Bixby he did not have the brains to become a pilot and that all he was good for was operating a bucket and mop. Bixby replied, "When I say I'll learn a man the river, I mean it. And you can depend on it, I'll learn him or kill him."

Once young Clemens had begun to feel more comfortable with the shape of the river, his next important lesson was to learn to *read* the water. He had

**A typical steamboat with its main features identified**

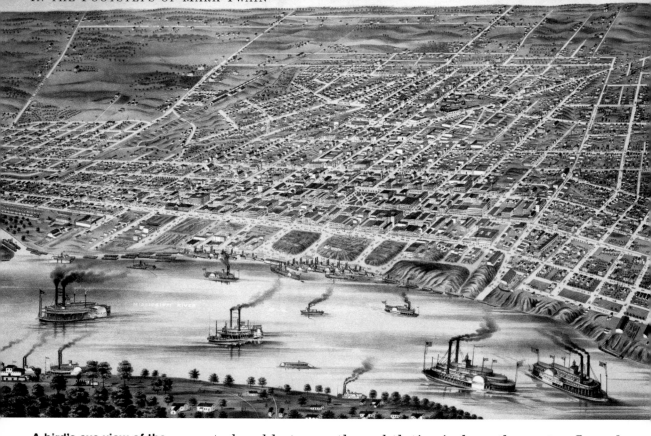

**A bird's eye view of the Mississippi port city of Memphis in 1870 (map reference 10)**

to be able to see the subtleties in how the water flowed on the surface to know what lurked beneath it. A long, slanting line on the face of the water meant a reef of rocks just beneath the surface; fine lines that branched out like a fan were an indication of little reefs; slick, greasy water on the surface could indicate a very shallow area; and so forth. The appearance of a small dimple on the surface of the water could mean a huge rock or old wreck that could tear apart the hull of the ship.

To test the young pilot, Bixby once left Clemens at the wheel for a familiar stretch, then hid behind a chimney when they approached an area Samuel was less familiar with. Clemens soon was so impressed with his own performance that he relaxed, started doing other work, and turned his back to the pilothouse window. When he turned to look out the window again, all he could see was what he thought was a large, underwater stone reef. He panicked, spinning the wheel and ringing the bells. Shortly afterward, Bixby stepped out from his hiding place and calmly showed young Clemens how to escape

## STEAMBOAT DAYS: IN THE WORDS OF MARK TWAIN

If I have seemed to love my subject, it is no surprising thing, for I loved the profession far better than any I have followed since, and I took a measureless pride in it. The reason is plain: a pilot, in those days, was the only unfettered and entirely independent human being that lived in the earth. Kings are but the hampered servants of parliament and people; parliaments sit in chains forged by their constituency; the editor of a newspaper cannot be independent, but must work with one hand tied behind him by party and patrons, and be content to utter only half or two-thirds of his mind; no clergyman is a free man and may speak the whole truth, regardless of his parish's opinions; writers of all kinds are manacled servants of the public. We write frankly and fearlessly, but then we 'modify' before we print. In truth, every man and woman and child has a master, and worries and frets in servitude; but in the day I write of, the Mississippi pilot had none. The captain could stand upon the hurricane deck, in the pomp of a very brief authority, and give him five or six orders while the vessel backed into the stream, and then that skipper's reign was over. The moment that the boat was under way in the river, she was under the sole and unquestioned control of the

pilot. He could do with her exactly as he pleased, run her when and whither he chose, and tie her up to the bank whenever his judgment said that that course was best. His movements were entirely free; he consulted no one, he received commands from nobody, he promptly resented even the merest suggestions. Indeed, the law of the United States forbade him to listen to commands or suggestions, rightly considering that the pilot necessarily knew better how to handle the boat than anybody could tell him. So here was the novelty of a king without a keeper, an absolute monarch who was absolute in sober truth and not by a fiction of words. I have seen a boy of eighteen taking a great steamer serenely into what seemed almost certain destruction, and the aged captain standing mutely by, filled with apprehension but powerless to interfere.

The pilothouse of riverboat with the pilot at the wheel

His interference, in that particular instance, might have been an excellent thing, but to permit it would have been to establish a most pernicious precedent. It will easily be guessed, considering the pilot's boundless authority, that he was a great personage in the old steamboating days. He was treated with marked courtesy by the captain and with marked deference by all the officers and servants; and this deferential spirit was quickly communicated to the passengers, too. I think pilots were about the only people I ever knew who failed to show, in some degree, embarrassment in the presence of traveling foreign princes. But then, people in one's own grade of life are not usually embarrassing objects.

the "imminent crash." Clemens remembered the event as one of several lasting lessons on the importance of not becoming complacent and overly confident. As it turned out, Clemens had panicked over nothing but a "wind reef"—that is, the illusion of a real reef caused by the wind. Clemens could have floated over it with ease—another lesson in knowing the subject well and trusting one's instincts.

Soon Clemens had indeed learned the river—shape, surface, and all. His education came at a cost, however. Because of the life-and-death necessity of constantly and accurately reading the Mississippi, the grace, beauty, and poetry of the river were lost to the young pilot. He ceased to enjoy the changes in light, season, and color of the majestic river. Instead, he saw that certain light meant poor weather the next day, a floating log meant a rising river, a slanting mark on the face of the water meant a reef that would destroy a boat, that lines and circles meant the water would become rapidly shallow, and that a gigantic old dying tree meant the loss of an important landmark soon. All things beautiful were simply gauged as useful tools for the safe handling of a riverboat.

Another important facet of Clemens's life on the river was the people he met. Gamblers, criminals, wealthy couples, slaves, and a countless cast of other characters paraded by Clemens on each trip up or down the river. He later commented that he never encountered a character in life or in fiction that he had not previously met on the river.

## Pilot Brown and Henry's Death

An event occurred during Clemens's training that affected him for life. Near the end of his apprenticeship, Clemens got his younger brother Henry hired aboard *The Pennsylvania* as a mud clerk. A mud clerk measured woodpiles and counted coal boxes. During the summer of 1858, the Clemens brothers served under Pilot William Brown, a "middle-aged, long, slim, bony, smooth-shaven, horse-faced, ignorant, stingy, malicious, snarling, fault-hunting, mote-magnifying tyrant" with an infallible memory. Clemens had served under Brown for several

Shown fishing here, the characters Tom Sawyer and the runaway slave Jim. It was the people that Clemens met—both as a child in Hannibal and in his youth on the Mississippi—that gave him models for the well-formed characters in his books.

months and thought he was the most ignorant, impatient, and abusive soul he had ever met.

Along the way Henry shouted a request for a plantation stop from the captain. Brown pretended not to hear Henry and breezed right on past the plantation. When questioned by the captain, Brown claimed Henry had never given him the information and verbally attacked Clemens when he told the captain that he had heard Henry shout the order.

About an hour later, Henry appeared in the pilothouse unaware of the incident. Brown angrily yelled at Henry and then ordered him to leave. When Henry turned his back on the pilot, Brown sprang after him with a lump of coal. To protect his brother, Samuel grabbed a stool and hit Brown with enough force to lay him out and then continued to beat him with his fists, taking out pent-up anger on the abusive pilot. Meanwhile, the steamboat traveled on down the river without a pilot at the wheel.

**A young boy holds the old riverboat pilot wheel of captain Sam Clemens in Hannibal, Missouri.**

Clemens had committed the ultimate crime for a pilot—one for which he could easily have lost his job. The captain called him aside and asked him about the incident. An honest accounting by Clemens of the confrontation led the captain to ask how severely Clemens had beaten the abusive pilot. When Samuel admitted that he had continued to pound him with his fists, the captain said, "I'm deuced glad of it! Hark ye, never mention that I said that. You have been guilty of a great crime; and don't you ever be guilty of it again, on this boat." The captain had been wishing for someone to stand up to Brown for some time.

**Samuel Clemens's riverboat pilot's license**

Nonetheless, Brown refused to serve on another boat with the Clemens brothers and demanded that one of them had to go. The captain fired Brown and wanted to hire Clemens as pilot, but Samuel did not feel he was ready for that level of responsibility. In the end, the captain had no choice but to rehire Brown for a final return trip upriver, where he intended to hire another pilot. Because Brown refused to work with Clemens, Samuel left *The Pennsylvania* for the return trip to St. Louis, but his brother stayed on. Samuel's new ship, the *A.T. Lacey*, followed *The Pennsylvania* up the river.

Shortly after the boats left the harbor (just south of Memphis, Tennessee), four of *The Pennsylvania*'s boilers exploded. More than 150 people (including Pilot Brown) were killed. Henry was blown into the water about 50 feet (15 m) from the wreckage but thought he was unhurt. In fact, he had breathed scalding air and severely damaged his lungs. Henry heard the passengers' screams and swam back to help the surviving women and children.

When Samuel's boat docked in Memphis about two days later, he discovered that his brother was dying from the lung damage. He sat with Henry for six days and nights. On the last day, a physician offered Clemens some hope for his brother's recovery, but during the night an incompetent intern administered a fatal dose of morphine to Henry. Clemens awoke from a fitful sleep to find his brother dead. Since Samuel had found Henry the job, he felt responsible fo

## STEAMBOAT DISASTERS: THE *ARABIA*

Life on the rivers in nineteenth-century United States was not easy. Disaster loomed around every bend of every river, and the boats themselves were not always safe. Countless riverboats sank throughout the Mississippi River basin, falling victim to floods, fires, boiler explosions, submerged obstacles, and collisions with other riverboats. Today, archaeologists and treasure hunters explore the wrecks as low water or changes in the river's course uncover them. One of the most fascinating riverboat wreck stories is that of the *Arabia*. In 1856, the steamer was traveling up the Missouri River just past Kansas City when it hit a giant tree trunk lodged in the river bottom. The tree punched a gaping hole in the boat, and it quickly sank. In 1987, the well-preserved wreck was discovered in a Kansas cornfield, about one-half mile (.8 km) from the current location of the Missouri. Portions of the boat and its contents can now be seen at the Arabia Steamboat Museum (map reference 1), which offers a fascinating glimpse into riverboat life during the same era that Mark Twain was traveling the nearby Mississippi.

his death and made a vow to become the safest riverboat pilot. Clemens's fight with Brown had likely saved his own life.

After studying the river for about two years, Clemens earned his pilot's license on April 9, 1859, and began working as a pilot on various vessels ranging from tiny tugs to *The City of Memphis*, then the largest and grandest steamboat on the river. By then he earned $250 a month—a grand salary at that time (about what the vice president of the United States earned) and more than his father had ever made. Since he had no real expenses on board the various boats he piloted, Clemens was able to send money home to help his mother. He also treated his mother to a riverboat trip to New Orleans in early 1861—"the grandest city she had ever seen."

Oddly enough, Clemens wrote very little about his experiences as a full-fledged pilot on the Mississippi. Perhaps he was such a good pilot that very little happened. In fact, *Life on the Mississippi* contains only a single, short paragraph about his two-year career as a licensed pilot. "Time drifted smoothly and prosperously on."

As Clemens's knowledge of the river grew, so did his propensity for stretching stories he told to other pilots. He soon became a popular onboard storyteller and was as at ease with passengers as he was with crew. He truly felt working on the river was his life's calling.

# CHAPTER 5

# THE START OF THE CIVIL WAR

Just as Clemens was easing into his life as a riverboat pilot—a life he felt he could continue forever—the winds of change were sweeping the nation. For decades, slavery had been a topic of controversy in the United States. This form of involuntary labor and the cruelty that went with it were beginning to attract the attention of numerous early human rights activists. Many of the industrialized Northern states no longer used—or even needed—slave labor. In the South, it was another story. Huge tobacco and cotton plantations depended on slave labor for their existence, and the mere mention of abolishing slavery was a rallying cry for seceding from the Union. The Southern states began to withdraw from the Union in 1861, and a war between the North and South appeared to be unavoidable.

Clemens was in New Orleans on January 26, 1861, when the state of Louisiana seceded. His ship steamed north the following morning. Clemens was able to celebrate his second anniversary as a licensed pilot on April 9, 1861, but just three days later, the first shots of the Civil War, fired at Fort Sumter, South Carolina, brought an abrupt end to Clemens's career as a riverboat pilot.

The Mississippi River was the commercial lifeline of the United States. From the start of the war, controlling the river was an important component of the Union plan for defeating the Confederacy. Controlling the entire length of the river would allow the Union to protect Northern cities from attack and cut off all supplies to Southern cities, crippling both their trade and their economies. The federal government soon halted all commercial traffic on the river and allowed only shipping related to the war effort. Then

**Union ironclad gunboat USS *Baron de Kalb*, originally named the USS *St. Louis***

The Union started military operations to capture Southern forts along the Mississippi. General Ulysses S. Grant almost single-handedly won the Civil War for the North with his brilliant western campaign that wrestled control of the Mississippi and its main tributaries from the South and cut the Confederacy into isolated pieces.

When war broke out, Samuel Clemens had a conflict. He was ordered to pilot an ironclad gunboat for the Union, but his sentiments at the time were more closely aligned with the South, and he knew he did not want to be a warship pilot. So he did not run the gunboat; he quit and went back to Hannibal on one of the last boats headed north. On the way (he was piloting the last riverboat north), cannon at the Jefferson Barracks near St. Louis fired twice on Clemens's vessel. The second shot smashed the glass of the pilothouse.

Clemens thought the war would last only a short time, and things would get back to normal, but he was wrong. Not only would the war last four years, but, by the time it ended, railroads were rapidly replacing riverboats. The glory years were over. By the time Clemens returned to the Mississippi more than two decades later, he was no longer a riverboat pilot but an accomplished author.

## THE MARION RANGERS

Soon after arriving in Hannibal after the closing of the Mississippi River, Samuel Clemens and some childhood buddies decided to form a unit of the Confederate Army— the new Marion Rangers (named for the county in which Hannibal is located). This unit, composed of a small group of local men, swore to be loyal to Missouri and drive all invaders from its soil. Like most young men of the time, Clemens and his buddies had an unrealistic idea of what war was like and thought of it as a game. They set off to locate an organized unit of the Confederate Army they could join. Along the way, they found a perfect spot to swim and fish, and that is what they did. Within two weeks, all zeal to become Confederate soldiers had faded away (the forced drills and marches were not very appealing), and they did not have enough ammunition to do much target practice. It rained. With the fun worn off (and word came that Union soldiers were looking for them), the Marion Rangers marched back to Hannibal and promptly disbanded—a move, Clemens noted later, that "was our finest decision."

# CHAPTER 6
# WANDERING OUT WEST

Seeing no immediate prospect of the end of the Civil War and not wishing to be forced to pilot a warship, Clemens considered change once again. Prior to the beginning of the war (when he lived in St. Louis), his brother Orion had worked for a lawyer named Edward Bates. When Abraham Lincoln became president, he named Bates attorney general of the United States. Bates, in turn, appointed Orion Clemens as secretary of the Territory of Nevada. Orion wanted his brother Samuel to become his own secretary. The younger Clemens eagerly agreed because it gave him a good reason to leave Missouri until the war ended.

In July 1861, the Clemens brothers headed west in a stagecoach bound for Nevada. Once they arrived in Carson City, the capital, they found there was very little for them to do other than a small amount of surveying from time to time. To fight boredom, the brothers (and others) regularly played cards in the saloon, where they also began another hobby—collecting scorpions and tarantulas in glass bottles that were then placed on shelves on the wall. One evening one of the men, Bob Howland, stumbled into the wall. The bottles crashed to the floor, releasing numerous scorpions and tarantulas into the room. Howland yelled, "Turn out boys! The tarantulas is loose!" The incident provided Clemens with one of many stories from this time period.

Because his job had very few responsibilities, Twain had plenty of time for storytelling, an art he truly began to hone. He also spent time looking for riches. He was going to stake a claim on the timber near Lake Tahoe, but he accidentally started a fire that snuffed out those chances. He and another friend found traces of a rich silver mine

During his time in Nevada, Samuel Clemens found plenty of time to write. He sent some of his stories to the *Territorial Enterprise* newspaper in Virginia City, Nevada, and was offered a full-time job as a city editor at the rate of $25 per week. He snapped up the offer. As he poked fun at politicians and told tall tales, Clemens used pen names. He signed some "Josh" for fun. On February 2, 1863, he began using the name "Mark Twain." The name came from his days as a riverboat pilot where "mark twain" (two fathoms) meant the point at the edge of safety. As Twain, Clemens felt he could use his wit effectively in "crusading journalism;" that is, he felt that by pointing out social and governmental problems, he could help bring about positive change. He soon became recognized throughout the West for his wit and wisdom. He was even challenged to a duel because of one of his jabs at a city leader, but he managed to talk his way out of it. Two private businesses in Virginia City are dedicated to keeping alive memories of Clemens's days in the area (map reference 13): The Mark Twain Bookstore was once a museum, and its walls are covered with artifacts from the Twain era. The Territorial Enterprise Museum is housed in the building that was the final location of the paper that Clemens once edited in Virginia City.

and intended to work it, but both were called away for other business, thinking the other remained to keep their stake on the claim. They left notes for each other and went their separate ways. When they returned, they found other men mining their claim and their hopes for riches dashed.

With no end to the Civil War in sight and his hopes of returning to the Mississippi River fading, Clemens spent the next few years writing and entertaining folks throughout the West. During this time, he met the entertainer Artemus Ward and promised him a story for an upcoming book.

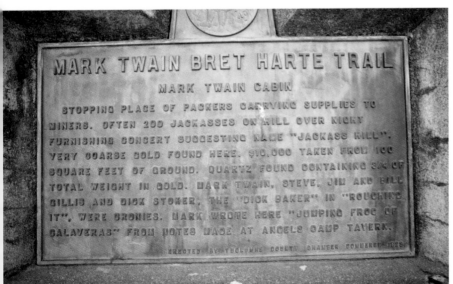

A sign marks a spot along the Mark Twain Bret Harte Trail on Jackass Hill near Columbia, California. Here Twain saw and wrote about two hundred donkeys pulling wagons over this pass each day, and he complained about the "wale of their chorus."

**Map showing the stages of Clemens's journey west**

Clemens moved to the San Francisco area in 1864, where he crossed paths with numerous other celebrities of the day, including literary greats Bret Harte and Ambrose Bierce. Harte helped him fine-tune his writing craft.

While in San Francisco, Clemens—now going by his pen name Mark Twain—decided to give prospecting another try. He headed for the hills with two friends to pan for gold. At night, they swapped stories. One particular tale, told by an old-timer named Ben Coon, was about a frog with unnatural jumping abilities. When Twain got back to San Francisco in 1865, he began writing more earnestly—and getting published. He also penned the

**Early photograph of Samuel Clemens with others as part of the Comstock delegation to the last territorial legislature of Nevada, in 1864**

story Coon had told, elaborated and expanded on it, and sent it to Ward for his book. The story was too late for the book, but Ward liked it so much he sent it on to New York's *Saturday Press*, where it was published November 18, 1865, as "Jim Smiley and the Jumping Frog." This story, later titled "The Celebrated Jumping Frog of Calaveras County," gave Twain his first major break as an author and is one of his best-known stories.

## Travels to Hawaii and Beyond

In early 1866, Twain convinced his editors at the *Sacramento Union* to send him to the Sandwich Islands (today called Hawaii) to work as a correspondent. He intended to write a special series of articles about the plantations. While on the islands, Twain tried his hand at surfing (with poor results), then an unknown sport to Americans. He also came upon an open boat carrying

A caricature of Mark Twain riding a jumping frog. The caricature is based on Twain's short story "The Celebrated Jumping Frog of Calaveras County" (1865).

### JUMPING FROG JUBILEE

Mark Twain's beloved tall tale about an amphibian with amazing legs is celebrated every year in the town in which the story is set. Angels Camp, California (map reference 2), held its first Jumping Frog Jubilee in 1928 as a way to raise money to pave its badly rutted dirt main street. Contestants showed up with frogs, and the one that jumped the farthest won a cash prize. The event became wildly popular—so much so that in 1933 the California Game and Fish Commission had to get involved to protect wild bullfrogs and ensure that they were being treated humanely. Today, the jubilee is held the third weekend in May in conjunction with the Calaveras County Fair. More than 2,000 frogs participate in a typical year, with the top fifty qualifying for the International Frog Jump Grand Finals. Rosie the Ribeter set the current world record jump of 21 feet, 5.5 inches (6.55 meters) in 1986. Any frog breaking this record will win a cash prize of five thousand dollars.

**Mark Twain "Enterprise" Building, C Street, Virginia City, Storey County, Nevada (map reference 7)**

**This serious study of humorist Samuel L. Clemens (center), before his hair and mustache turned white, was made by photographer Levin C. Handy. Flanking Clemens are George A. Townsend (*left*), war correspondent, novelist, poet, and playwright, and David Gray, editor of the *Buffalo Courier*.**

fifteen starving passengers. Their ship had burned, leaving them adrift for forty-three days. The story he filed, based on the survivors' stories, caused a stir. When Twain returned to San Francisco, a friend encouraged him to become a lecturer and to tell his stories from the Sandwich Islands to audiences (just as Artemus Ward did with other tales). Twain pondered this seriously and then took to the stage, thinking one more foolish thing in his life would not matter.

On October 2, 1866, the Academy of Music in San Francisco was packed with people waiting to hear Twain speak. The posters promised: "Doors open at 7 O'Clock. The Trouble Will Start at 8." His dry delivery of humorous tales was an immediate smashing success. In May 1867, Twain's first book, *The Celebrated Jumping Frog of Calaveras County and Other Sketches*, was published. He was well on his way to success.

After the release of his book (and successful sales), Twain convinced the *Alta California*, a newspaper, to finance a five-month trip to Europe and North Africa in

exchange for stories based on his observations. He filed stories from France, Italy, Greece, Egypt, and the Holy Land, and described the numerous people he met while traveling. These stories were eventually published as the book *Innocents Abroad*. It was on this trip that he met Charles Langdon, who carried a portrait of a beautiful young woman painted on ivory. Langdon promised to introduce Twain to the woman—his sister, Olivia—when they got back. Twain was smitten with Olivia, who was overwhelmed by the man and his drinking, smoking, swearing, and gambling habits. He promised to change if she would marry him. She eventually did, on February 2, 1870.

Twain performing on stage in 1877

## MARK TWAIN ON STAGE

Samuel Clemens—as Mark Twain—was almost as popular during his life for his entertaining stage shows as for his books. During these "lectures," Twain would regale his appreciative audiences with several of his popular humorous tales. He remained an active and wildly popular lecturer for much of his life; more than once, the stage tours rescued him from financial problems caused by questionable investments.

Today, several Twain impersonators offer shows modeled on the famous author's lectures, but the best-known is actor Hal Holbrook. He started playing Twain on stage in 1954 and found fame in 1959 with his show *Mark Twain Tonight*. The production moved to Broadway in 1966; he soon won a Tony Award for his portrayal of Twain. The show is still periodically in production, and Holbrook has given more than two thousand performances, drawing on the huge body of Twain stories to create a new and different show each time. *Mark Twain Tonight*, a popular DVD, is also an entertaining introduction to one of the master storytellers of the United States.

# CHAPTER 7

# BECOMING A CONNECTICUT YANKEE

As a wedding gift, Olivia's father gave the couple a three-story brick mansion in Buffalo, New York, and lent Twain enough money to become part owner of the *Buffalo Express* newspaper. After spending a year in Buffalo, Twain and "Livy" sold their home and interest in the paper and moved to Hartford, Connecticut, to be closer to his publisher. By 1872, *Innocents Abroad* had sold more than 100,000 copies and had made Twain popular all across the country. Even commercial products, such as sewing machines and cigars, were being named after the author/lecturer.

Despite his popularity, critics in the United States felt Twain's work was "lightweight" and "cute" and did not take him seriously as an author. Following the age-old advice of writing what he knew, Twain began to write about his western adventures in *Roughing It*, and he continued to be a successful lecturer as well. It was not, however, until Twain began writing about what he truly knew and loved—his life on the Mississippi River—that his career took off.

Before that happened, however, Twain's life was affected by other events. In August 1870, Livy's father died, and just three months later, the couple's first child, Langdon, was born prematurely. The boy, Twain's only son, died in June 1872. The events changed Twain. He became disillusioned and disgusted by popular novels and teamed up with his neighbor, Charles Dudley Warner, to write *The Gilded Age*, an attack on crime and corruption in the post-Civil War government. It was published in 1873 and became a bestseller.

With the wealth generated by his successes, Twain built a huge mansion in Hartford. The unusual house had

Mark Twain's unique house in Hartford, Connecticut—a home the family occupied from 1874 to 1891—was designated a National Historic Landmark in 1963 (map reference 6). A massive restoration project was completed in 1974. During the 1990s, the scope of the museum was greatly expanded, and a new exhibition building was completed. Today, the museum complex continues to grow and is a fitting tribute to one of the world's greatest writers. It is a popular tourist destination, hosting more than sixty thousand visitors each year, and it offers a variety of educational programs about Twain's life and writing.

Three chimneys, gables, and a balcony rise from the roof of the architecturally eccentric home of Mark Twain. The house was built in 1881 for the huge sum of one hundred thousand dollars.

orches, turrets, huge hallways, a conservatory with lants, a billiard room, and an office that jutted out rom the mansion like a Mississippi River steamboat's ilothouse. Here the Clemens entertained and began aising a family. First came Susan Olivia, then Clara, and inally Jean. Twain was in love with his daughters and avished attention and gifts on them. His newfound wealth nd fame also marked a return of his smoking, drinking, wearing, and gambling habits, all of which he had given p when he married. One of these forms of gambling— nvesting in inventions (his own and others')—eventually rove him to the brink of bankruptcy.

*Above:* Clara Clemens

*Right:* Etched portrait of Samuel Clemens with daughters Clara and Susie

## Writing about the Mississippi

Mark Twain grew up in Missouri, where many people owned slaves, and he spent considerable time with the slaves on his uncle's farm. His association allowed Twain to learn a great deal about slaves and their culture, but it appears that early in his life he held the racist attitudes that were typical of Southerners at that time. Still, he was deeply affected by the violence he saw inflicted on slaves, especially the murder of an innocent slave by a white man that he witnessed in Hannibal in 1845. After the Civil War

## MARK TWAIN IN ELMIRA, NEW YORK

Samuel Clemens's wife, Olivia Langdon, graduated from Elmira College in 1864, and the Clemens family spent many summers in the Elmira area, just south of the Finger Lakes. It is not surprising that this small school has become one of the world's leading centers for Mark Twain research. The college's Center for Mark Twain Studies (map reference 3) maintains a significant archive of Twain papers, plus an exhibit of photos, furniture, clothing, and other memorabilia from the nearby Quarry Farm home (now owned by the college). In addition, Mark Twain's unique octagonal study from Quarry Farm—in which he wrote portions of several of his greatest works—was moved to the campus in 1952. Twain and his family are buried in Elmira's Woodlawn Cemetery.

**Olivia's family home in Elmira, New York**

'wain started to wonder whether the institutions for vhich the South so valiantly fought were worth the ost of so many lives.

In 1874, driven by his unresolved feelings toward lavery, Twain wrote "A True Story." It was told in the oice of an exslave and based on the experiences of Aunty Cord, a slave cook at Livy's sister's farm. The story was

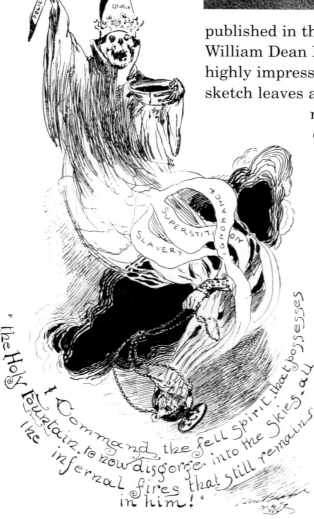

published in the *Atlantic* magazine that November. William Dean Howells, a famous critic of the day, was highly impressed and wrote, "the rugged truth of the sketch leaves all other stories of slave life far behind and reveals a gift in the author for the simple, dramatic report of reality which we have seen equaled in no other American writer."

Having now begun to examine his past (and having been recognized for it), Twain invented the town of St. Petersburg (based on Hannibal) and thought up the characters Tom Sawyer (with much of his own personality), Becky Thatcher (much like Laura Hawkins), Huck Finn (who resembled Tom Blankenship), and Aunt Polly (who was very much like an older version of his own mother). He filled the book *Tom Sawyer* with swimming, cave exploration, skipping school, rafting, whitewashing the fence, and many other adventures. Twain's secret recipe for fine fiction was to take his own life (what he knew best) and combine it with observations on the human condition. The resulting eternal truths hit a sympathetic chord with millions of people. Most of

Twain's writing during this time was done either in Hartford or at Quarry Farm (near Elmira, New York), where Livy's sister lived.

In 1872, Twain went on a lecture tour to Europe and visited England for the first time. The trip led to *A Tramp Abroad* and *The Prince and the Pauper*, and ultimately inspired his much later work, *A Connecticut Yankee in King Arthur's Court*.

**Mark Twain at home in bed**

# CHAPTER 8
# FINAL YEARS

During Twain's later years, his fortunes ebbed and flowed. His attempts at writing plays did poorly, but each time a new book was released, people clamored to buy it. In 1883 Twain's *Life on the Mississippi*, a fictionalized account of his time learning to become a riverboat pilot, was published. Two years later Twain brought back his beloved *Tom Sawyer* characters in *The Adventures of Huckleberry Finn*, still recognized as one of the greatest novels ever written.

*The Adventures of Huckleberry Finn* was told in the voice of that character and was one of the first novels written in common speech. The book follows "Huck" Finn as he runs away from difficult home life and floats on a raft down the Mississippi River with an escaped slave named Jim. It is a story filled with colorful characters and a strong message about freedom, but it is probably best know for its blunt examination of slavery and racism.

Critics praised the book as "true American writing," but it remains one of the most controversial novels ever published. The book was unpopular with whites in parts of the South because they felt they were depicted as petty and cruel. Other critics, not seeming to understand Twain's message, have accused the author of racism, in part because of his use of common language that included racial slurs.

The same year that *The Adventures of Huckleberry Finn* was published, Twain set up a publishing company called Charles L. Webster and Company. It would publish his and other works, including the memoirs of Ulysses S. Grant, Union Civil War general and president of the United States for two terms following the war. Twain helped Grant write his memoirs. The manuscript was finished four days before

In the early 1870s, Mark Twain wanted to write an account of his piloting days on the Mississippi River to help preserve the memory of the rapidly disappearing steamboat era. This account became *Old Times on the Mississippi*, a serial that was published in seven installments in the *Atlantic Monthly* magazine in 1875. This work eventually became chapters four to seventeen of the book *Life on the Mississippi*. For the effort, Twain enlisted publisher James Osgood and stenographer Roswell Phelps to accompany him on a return trip down the Mississippi River to refresh his memory and to gather additional information for the book.

It is interesting to note that a chapter that was considered insulting to Southerners was omitted from the serial version at the last minute. The deleted chapter was eventually released in 1913 (after Twain's death) as *The Suppressed Chapter of Life on the Mississippi*. Originally published in 1883, *Life on the Mississippi* offers many things to the reader. First and foremost, it is nonfiction disguised as fiction. Clemens, in the voice of Mark Twain, really was writing about his own life (though details were embellished for the story). The book serves as a memoir, a travel guide, and a group of short stories that introduce readers to geography, history, human nature, folklore, and scores of fascinating details. A short three-chapter introduction tells the basic geography and history of the Mississippi River. The next seventeen chapters—almost one-third of the book—detail young Samuel Clemens's experiences as a cub steamboat pilot, learning his trade under the guidance of Horace Bixby. He also recalls the abuse of Pilot Brown and the explosion of the steamboat *The Pennsylvania*, which killed at least 150 people, including his brother Henry. Oddly enough, and as detailed as the other information is, Clemens devotes only a single short paragraph to his two years as a licensed Mississippi steamboat pilot.

The remainder of *Life on the Mississippi* describes Twain's return to the river after twenty-one years, along with all the accompanying changes, including the decline of trade. He and his partners set out downstream from St. Louis on a packet steamer named the *Gold Dust*. Twain soon discovered that Robert Styles, the packet steamer's pilot, was a cub pilot at the same time as Twain. He also mentions that the *Gold Dust* exploded a few months after their trip, in August 1882, killing several people.

**First editions of Mark Twain's books about the Mississippi River**

**Mark Twain in academic robes receiving an honorary degree from Oxford University, England**

the general died. Twain personally edited the book, which became a huge bestseller. However, the company invested unwisely in typesetting machinery and soon faced severe financial problems. The company failed in 1894, leaving Twain with a debt of nearly one hundred thousand dollars.

During this period, in 1891, Twain moved his family to Europe, and they spent much of the final decade of the century out of the United States. Twain's need for money forced him to set out on a "world" lecture tour through the western United States, Canada, Australia, New Zealand, India, and South Africa. He was in poor health and reluctant to return to the road, but he felt that this was his best route to financial stability. The tour was a huge success. It ended after eighteen months and more than one hundred performances, and he reportedly earned enough money to pay off nearly half of his debt.

Over the next several years, Twain was able to put himself back on secure financial footing, but during this time he experienced great personal loss. His daughter Susan died of meningitis in August 1895. His wife Livy also became seriously ill and died in 1904.

In 1902, Twain was invited back to Hannibal, Missouri, to hand out diplomas to graduating high school seniors. During his address, he stated, "My own bottom still tingles from the switchings I received from my teachers. Now I'm handing out diplomas. Life takes some strange turns indeed." During this final visit, the sixty-six-year-old author, dressed all in white, visited his childhood home and piloted a riverboat one last time.

Twain wanted to write one last book before he died: his autobiography. It was his plan that it would not be published

SAMUEL L.
CLEMENS
"MARK TWAIN"
1835 – 1910
American Writer
lived here in
1896-7

LONDON COUNTY COUNCIL

*Above:* A London County Council plaque marks the former residence, between 1896 and 1897, of Samuel Clemens in London, England.

*Right:* Mark Twain sits in a rocker on the front porch of his family home, enjoying a cigar. The annotated photograph was one in a series for which the author and humorist provided a description—August 29, 1906, Dublin, New Hampshire.

*Below:* Map showing the route of Twain's U.S. tour

until after his death so it would be completely truthful. The *North American Review* magazine, however, offered Twain thirty thousand dollars just to publish the beginning of the book. He accepted the offer and used the money to build a new summer house in Redding, Connecticut, where he could live with his two remaining daughters.

Sadly, events conspired to disrupt Twain's plans for his final years. First, his daughter Clara was married in November 1909 and moved out of the house. Then, only one month later, his daughter Jean suffered a heart attack and died. Twain was alone. He had earlier stated, "I came in with Halley's Comet in 1835. It is coming again next

*Above:* Caricature of Mark Twain following Clemens's announcement that he intended to leave the United States.

*Right:* Writer Mark Twain relaxes on a ship deck with his feet on the railings, March 15, 1901.

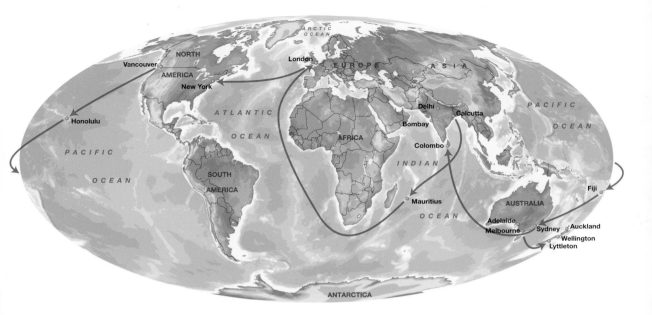

year, and I expect to go out with it. It will be the greatest disappointment of my life if I don't go out with Halley's Comet. The Almighty has said, no doubt: 'Now here are these two unaccountable freaks; they came in together, they must go out together.'"

Samuel Clemens—Mark Twain—died April 21, 1910, the day after Comet Halley reached perihelion, the point closest to the sun.

*Above:* **Map showing the route of Twain's world tour**

*Below:* **This image was shown during a celebration honoring the "two-timers," who saw Halley's Comet in 1910 and 1986. Clemens. of course, was an earlier two-timer.**

# CHAPTER 9
# MARK TWAIN'S LEGACY

During his lifetime, Mark Twain may have been the world's best-known celebrity in the United States. Why is he still so important—and popular—nearly one hundred years after his death? A simple answer may be that he was a great writer, and his stories and books are every bit as entertaining today as when they were written. There is more, however, to the Twain legacy than the body of literature he produced.

In many ways, Mark Twain was an embodiment of quite a few of the best parts of the American spirit. He was an adventurer and traveler, crisscrossing the United States and the globe throughout his lifetime, always looking for opportunities to explore new places. Twain was also a goodwill ambassador who easily connected with people from other cultures. Although he remained very much an American, he was comfortable socializing with, and living among, people in other countries. Mark Twain was a hard worker who never shirked his responsibilities. He never shied away from taking on a difficult job—even late in life when he was immensely popular—if he felt that it was the right thing to do.

Probably even more important than Twain's exploration of the world was his exploration of some of the most difficult questions facing U.S. society. Although he could have made a comfortable living writing light humor, he instead used his intellect and writing talent to attack some of the evils he saw in the world. Twain was an outspoken critic of government corruption. Later, he used his writing to protest U.S. military activities around the world, and he was openly opposed to the United States's bloody takeover of the Philippines. Most significant, though, was the way

Twain opened U.S. eyes to racism, especially through the pages of his greatest novel, *The Adventures of Huckleberry Finn.* Some people still try to ban the book from municipal and school libraries, which points to the power of its words. Mark Twain—Samuel Clemens—was a man who believed in Americans, but he was not afraid to challenge us all to be better people.

**Right:** Mark Twain's grave in Woodlawn Cemetery, Elmira, New York. His son-in law's name and portrait are also on the plaque.

**Below:** The captain works in the bridge of the riverboat, *Mark Twain*, on the Mississippi, in Hannibal, Missouri.

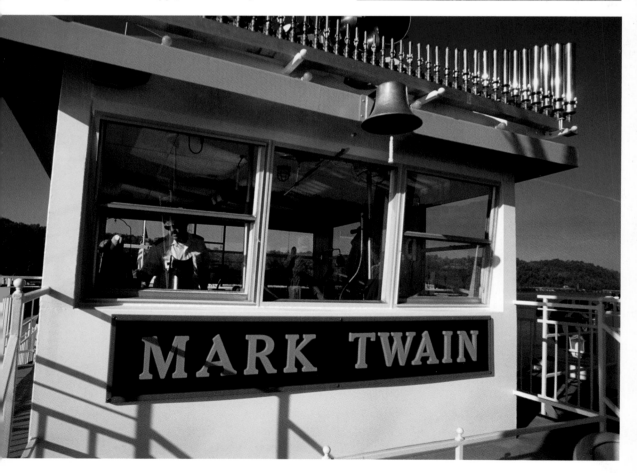

# Places to Visit and Research

Many sites crucial to Mark Twain and the Mississippi River can be researched online or visited. Below is a list in alphabetical order of some of those historic sites, parks, museums, and houses, along with their addresses, telephone numbers, and Web sites. Places described in the sidebars are shown with green dots on the map on pages 6 and 59.

**1 Arabia Steamboat Museum**
400 Grand Boulevard, Kansas City, MO 64106. (816) 471-4030.
www.1856.com. See page 35.

**2 Calaveras County Fair & Jumping Frog Jubilee**
P.O. Box 489, Angels Camp, CA 95222-0489. (209) 736-2561.
www.frogtown.org. See page 41.

**3 Center For Mark Twain Studies, Elmira College**
One Park Place, Elmira, NY 14901. (607) 735-1941.
www.elmira.edu/academics/ar_marktwain.shtml. See page 47.

**4 Delta Queen Steamboat Company**
Robin Street Wharf, 1380 Port of New Orleans Place, New Orleans, LA 70130. (504) 586-0631.
www.deltaqueen.com. See page 21.

**5 Mark Twain Birthplace State Historical Site**
37352 Shrine Road, Stoutsville, Mo 65283-9722. (573) 565-3449.
www.mostateparks.com/twainsite.htm. See page 11.

**6 The Mark Twain House and Museum**
351 Farmington Avenue, Hartford, CT 06105. (860) 247-0998.
www.marktwainhouse.org.
See page 45.

**7 Mark Twain Bookstore**
111 South C Street, Virginia City, NV 89440. (775) 847-0454.
www.marktwainbooks.com.
See page 42.

**8 Mark Twain State Park**
20057 State Park Road Office, Stoutsville, MO 65283.
(573) 565-3440
www.mostateparks.com/twainpark.htm. See page 11.

**9 Mark Twain's Boyhood Home and Museum**
208 Hill Street, Hannibal, MO 63401-3316. (573) 221-9010.
www.marktwainmuseum.org/.
See page 13-16, 18.
**Hannibal has a special historic district that includes Twain's home, John M. Clemen's Law Office, Becky Thatcher House, and various Twain-related statues and monuments. Related local attractions include steamboat rides and "Mark Twain's Cave."**

**10 Mississippi River Museum**
Mud Island River Park, 125 North Front Street, Memphis, TN 38103.
(901) 576-7241
www.memphistravel.com/mississippi_river_museum.asp.
See page 30.
**Popular museum features 5,000 artifacts in eighteen galleries educating visitors about the history,**
biology, transportation, and culture associated with the Mississippi.

**11 National Mississippi River Museum and Aquarium**
350 East 3rd Street, Dubuque, Iowa 52001. (563) 557-9545.
www.mississippirivermuseum.com.
See page 9.

**12 Science Museum of Minnesota**
120 West Kellogg Boulevard, St. Paul, MN 55102. (651) 221-4585.
www.smm.org. See page 27.

**13 Territorial Enterprise Museum**
23 South C Street, Virginia City, 89440. (775) 847-0525
www.cr.nps.gov/nr/travel/nevada/ter.htm. See page 39.

*Right:* **This map shows the location of the places identified in the Places to Visit and Research section. The green dots indicate places mentioned in sidebars.**

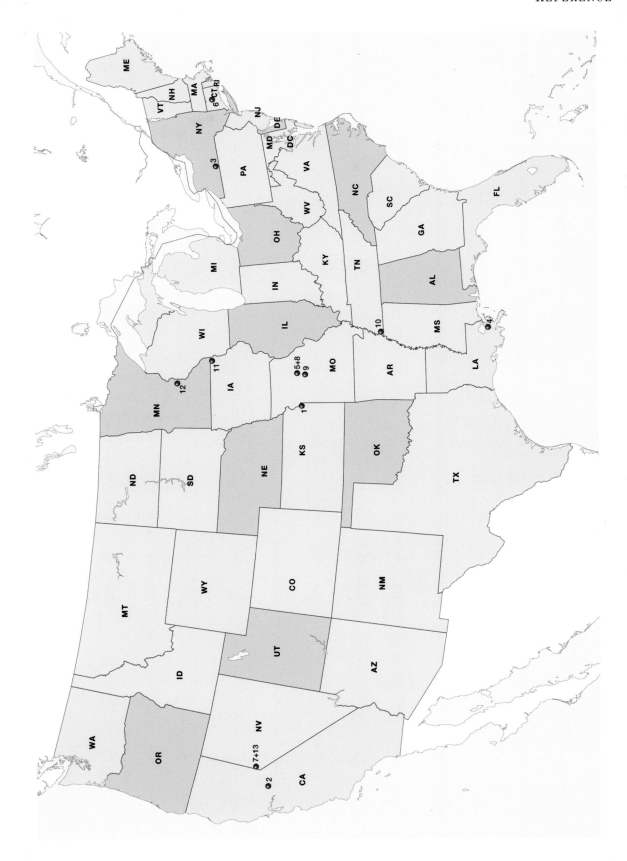

# Time Line

**1835**
Samuel Clemens is born November 30 in Florida, Missouri. Halley's Comet is clearly visible in the sky.

**1839**
Clemens family moves to Hannibal, Missouri.

**1847**
Samuel's father, John Clemens, dies on March 24.

**1848**
Samuel begins printer apprenticeship under Joseph P. Ament.

**1851**
Clemens's first-known work, "A Gallant Fireman," is published in his brother's paper.

**1853–1857**
Clemens works as a printer in St. Louis, Missouri; New York, New York; Philadelphia, Pennsylvania, Keokuk, Iowa; and Cincinnati, Ohio.

**1857**
Clemens leaves Cincinnati, bound for Brazil. He convinces Horace Bixby to train him as riverboat pilot.

**1859**
Clemens becomes licensed as pilot, April 9.

**1861**
Clemens leaves the river when Union gunboats close the Mississippi to commercial traffic; trains with Confederate volunteer group, the Marion Rangers, for about two weeks; travels with his brother Orion to Carson City, Nevada, by stagecoach.

**1862**
Clemens becomes a reporter and freelance writer for the *Territorial Enterprise* newspaper in Virginia City, Nevada.

**1863**
Clemens signs his name as "Mark Twain" for the first time.

**1864**
Clemens becomes a reporter for the *San Francisco Morning Call* newspaper.

**1866**
Clemens spends four months in Hawaii.

**1867**
Clemens sets sail for Europe and the Holy Land.

**1870**
Clemens marries Olivia Langdon on February 2; first child and only son, Langdon, is born November 7.

**1871**
Samuel and Olivia move to Hartford, Connecticut.

**1872**
Susan Clemens born March 19; Langdon Clemens dies in June.

**1874**
Clara Clemens born in June.

**1876**
*The Adventures of Tom Sawyer* published.

**1878–1879**
Clemens travels with family to Europe.

**1880**
Jean Clemens born July 26.

**1882**
Clemens takes two-month boat trip on the Mississippi.

**1883**
*Life on the Mississippi* published.

**1884**
*Adventures of Huckleberry Finn* published.

**1891**
Clemens family moves to Europe and stays for most of the next ten years.

**1894**
Twain's publishing house declares bankruptcy.

**1895–1896**
Clemens embarks on round-the-world lecture trip to repay creditors.

**1896**
Susan Clemens dies August 18.

**1900**
Clemens family returns from Europe.

**1904**
Olivia Clemens dies June 5.

**1908**
Clemens moves to Stormfield in Redding, Connecticut.

**1909**
Clara Clemens marries Ossip Gabrilowitsch; Jean Clemens dies December 23; Clemens predicts his own death with the next appearance of Halley's Comet.

**1910**
Halley's Comet visible February though July; Samuel Clemens dies April 21.

# Glossary

**Alamo** Famed fortress in San Antonio, Texas, besieged and taken by Mexican troops in 1836 during the war for Texan independence.

**amphibian** A large class of animals with cold blood, including frogs and salamanders.

**apprentice** A person (usually a young boy) who works and often lives with a master craftsman to learn his trade.

**autobiography** An account of a person's life written by that person.

**bankruptcy** When a person or a company is legally declared by a court to be unable to pay their debts.

**bumpkin** A clumsy or awkward country dweller, often perceived by town or city people as stupid or unsophisticated.

**Confederacy** The Southern states that left the country to be independent and maintain their agricultural style of life and economy, which depended heavily on the labor of slaves. Opposed by the Union States in the North that fought to bring the Confederate states back into the country during the Civil War.

**constituency** A group of citizens in a given area that is entitled to elect somebody to represent them in a legislature or other governing body.

**correspondent** A person who is employed by a newspaper to write regular reports for publication, often about a specific event taking place at a distant location.

**daguerreotype** An early photograph using silver plates instead of film or computer recording of images; developed in the mid-nineteenth century and replaced by simpler methods soon thereafter.

**editor** Someone who runs or manages a newspaper or some part of it, deciding on content, style, and other matters.

**fathom** A unit of measurement equal to 6 feet (1.8 meters) that is used to determine the depth of water.

**frontier** The edge or end of known territory; in the U.S., the West.

**Halley's Comet** A comet, usually visible to the naked eye, that returns near the earth about every seventy-six years. Its return on this schedule was first predicted in the 1700s by Edmond Halley, for whom the comet was named.

**heyday** Peak time of success or prosperity.

**Holy Land** A region on the eastern shore of the Mediterranean Sea, now consisting of Israel and Palestine, that is revered by Jews, Muslims, and Christians.

**homage** Respectful remarks.

**hull** The main body of a boat, including the bottom, sides, and deck.

**Industrial Revolution** The major shift in the economy and society from an agricultural to manufacturing basis; in Europe it happened in the eighteenth and nineteenth centuries, while in the United States it came mainly in the nineteenth century and later to most of the rest of the world.

**lecture** A presentation given by a speaker to inform an audience about a topic. Today lectures are usually associated with education, such as when a professor gives a lecture to a classroom of students. In the nineteenth century, lectures were a popular form of entertainment and often involved the speaker telling humorous stories.

**lock** An enclosed section of a river or canal that is used to transfer a boat between two waterways with different levels. The boat enters the lock, and gates are closed behind it. Then water is pumped in to raise the boat or pumped out to lower the boat. Afterward the gates are reopened, and the boat exits the lock.

**Mississippi River** The United States' greatest river and most important commercial waterway. Flowing 2,300 miles (37,000 kilometers) from Lake Itasca, Minnesota, to the Gulf of Mexico near New Orleans, Louisiana, the river's watershed drains more than 1.2 million square miles (3.1 square kilometers), or about 41 percent of the lower forty-eight states.

**molasses** A thick, dark syrup that comes from the refining of sugar or other crops and is used in many foods and animal feeds, as well as to produce rum.

**packet steamer** A mail, freight, or passenger boat that runs on a fixed course and schedule.

**paddle wheeler** A boat moved by a large side or rear wheel with broad plates or paddles to push against the water. Often powered by steam engines in Twain's day.

**pen name** An assumed name used by an author instead of their real name. Mark Twain was Samuel Clemens's pen name. Also known as a pseudonym or a nom de plume.

**pilot (riverboat)** A person who is trained and licensed to guide a boat through a particular stretch of river. He or she is responsible for learning all the potential hazards of that river and to avoid them. Not to be confused with the captain, who was the "boss" of a boat.

**plantation** A farm, usually large and often in the South; in Twain's time, place where slaves labored to grow tobacco, cotton, or other crops.

**printing press** A machine used to print newspapers, books, flyers, or other publications by transferring ink to sheets of paper. The first press was invented in Germany by Johann Gutenberg in the 1450s.

**saloon** A bar or dancehall.

**secede** To leave or formally depart from an agreement, such as the Constitution that formed the United States. Southern states seceded from the Union at the start of the Civil War (1861–1865).

**shoal** An area of shallow water caused by a sandbar or rock outcropping that is difficult to see and hazardous to boats. Sometimes called a reef.

**slavery** The ownership of another person as property; slavery in the United States was confined largely to the South in Twain's time and had become very controversial. Believed essential for the labor-intensive agriculture of the South but believed equally immoral in the North, it led in part to the Civil War (1861–1865).

**spittoon** A bowl or jar into which tobacco chewers and others spit.

**steamboat** A boat that is powered by a steam engine. This term is most commonly associated with the nineteenth-century riverboats that were usually propelled by a paddle wheel fitted on the stern.

**stenographer** A person who is employed to write down or type dictation or conversation.

**stern** The rear part of a boat.

**tall tale** A type of story, popular in the Old West, that purposely uses colorful characters, humor, and exaggeration to explain a natural phenomenon or some person's special skills. Paul Bunyan and Pecos Bill are two well-known characters from tall tales. Many tall tales originated in bragging contests that were common in mining, logging, and other frontier camps.

**vignette** A short piece of writing or part of one, often descriptive of one person or event.

**watch** A turn on duty, especially for a ship's crew.

**wind reef** A ripple or pattern of waves in water that resembles a shoal or other obstacle but is in fact just the effect of air.

# Further Resources

## Books

Aller, Susan Bivin, *Biography: Mark Twain* (A&E). Minneapolis: Lerner Publications Co., 2001

Collins, David R., *Mark T-W-A-I-N! A Story about Samuel Clemens.* Minneapolis: Carolrhoda Books Inc., 1994

North, Sterling, *Mark Twain and the River*. Boston: Houghton Mifflin Co., 1961

Powers, Ron, *Dangerous Water: A Biography of the Boy Who Became Mark Twain.* New York: Basic Books, 1999

Rasmussen, R. Kent, *Mark Twain For Kids, His Life & Times.* Chicago: Chicago Review Press, 2004

Twain, Mark, *Life on the Mississippi*. New York: Oxford University Press, 1996

Twain, Mark, *Mark Twain's Autobiography*. New York: P.F. Collier and Son, 1925

Ward, Geoffrey C., Dayton Duncan, and Ken Burns, *Twain, An Illustrated* Biography. New York: Alfred A Knopf, 2001

## Web Sites

Mark Twain: A Look at the Life and Works of Samuel Clemens
www.hannibal.net/twain

The Mark Twain House & Museum
www.marktwainhouse.org

Mark Twain in His Times
etext.lib.virginia.edu/railton/index2 html

Mark Twain Quotations
www.twainquotes.com

Twain Web (Mark Twain Forum)
www.york.ca/twainweb

Twaintimes
www.twaintimes.net/page1.htm

# Index

**Bold numbers indicate illustrations.**

3430